Pandosto: Or, the Historie of Dorastus and Fawnia

Robert Greene

⁌ THE TRIUMPH

OF TIME

WHEREIN IS DISCOVERED

by a pleasant Historie, that although by the meanes
of sinister fortune, Truth may be concealed
yet by Time in spight of fortune it
is most manifestly reuealed.

Pleasant for age to auoyde drowsie thoughtes,
profitable for youth to eschue other wanton
pastimes, and bringing to both a desired content.

Temporis filia veritas.

⁌ By Robert Greene, Maister of Artes
in Cambridge.

Omne tulit punctum qui miscuit vtile dulci.

Imprinted at London by Thomas Orwin for Thomas
Cadman, dwelling at the Signe of the Bible,
neere vnto the North doore of Paules,

1588.

21·XII·20·

TO THE GENTLEMEN READERS HEALTH.
The paultring Poet Aphranius, being blamed for troublinge
the Emperor Trajan with so many doting Poems, adventured
notwithstanding, stil to present him with rude and homely
verses, excusing himselfe with the courtesie of the Emper-
our, which did as friendly accept, as he fondly offerd. So
Gentlemen, if any condemne my rashnesse for troubling
your eares with to many unlearned Pamphlets: I will straight
shroud my selfe under the shadowe of your courtesies, and
with Aphranius lay the blame on you as well for frendly
reading them, as on my selfe for fondly penning them: Hoping though fond curious, or rather currish backbiters breathe
out slaunderous speeches: yet the courteous Readers (whom
I feare to offend) wil requite my travell, at the least with
silence: and in this hope I rest

wishing you health and happines.

ROBERT GREENE.

1

🙰🙰 TO THE RIGHT HONORABLE GEORGE CLIF-
FORD, EARLE OF CUMBERLAND, ROBERT GREENE
WISHETH INCREASE OF HONOUR AND VERTUE.
The Rascians (right honorable) when by long gazing against
the Sunne, they become halfe blinde, recover their sightes
by looking on the blacke Loade-stone. Unicornes being glutted with brousing on roots of Licquoris, sharpen their stom-
acks with crushing bitter grasse. ❡ Alexander vouchsafed
as well to smile at the croked picture of Vulcan, as to wonder
at the curious counterfeite of Venus. The minde is sometimes
delighted as much with small trifles as with sumptuous triumphs; and as wel pleased with hearing of Pans homely fancies, as of Hercules renowmed laboures. ❡ Syllie Baucis
coulde not serve Jupiter in a silver plate, but in a woodden
dish. Al that honour Esculapius, decke not his shrine with
Iewels. Apollo gives Oracles as wel to the poor man for his
mite, as to the rich man for his treasure. The stone Echites is
not so much liked for the colour, as for vertue, and giftes are
not to be measured by the worth, but by the will. Mison that
unskilfull Painter of Greece, adventured to give unto Darius
the shielde of Pallas, so roughlie shadowed, as he smiled
more at the follie of the man, then at the imperfection of his
arte. So I present unto your honour the triumph of time, so
rudelie finished, as I feare your honour wil rather frowne
at my impudencie, then laugh at my ignorancie: But I hope
my willing minde shal excuse my slender skill, and your
honours curtesie shadowe my rashnes. ❡ They which feare
the biting of vipers do carie in their hands the plumes of a
Phœnix. Phydias drewe Vulcan sitting in a chair of Ivory.
Cæsars crow durst never cry, Ave, but when she was pearked
on the Capitoll. And I seeke to shroude this imperfect Pam-
phlet under your honours patronage, doubting the dint of
such invenomed vipers, as seeke with their slaunderous reproches to carpe at al, being oftentimes, most unlearned of
all; and assure myselfe, that your honours renowmed val-
ure, and vertuous disposition shall be a sufficient defence to
protect me from the Poysoned tongues of such scorning
Sycophants, hoping that as Jupiter vouchsafed to lodge in

2

Philemons thatched Cotage: and Phillip of Macedon, to take a bunche of grapes of a country pesant, so I hope your honour, measuring my worke by my will, and wayghing more the mind than the matter, will when you have cast a glaunce at this toy, with Minerva, under your golden Target couer a deformed Owle. And in this hope I rest, wishing unto you, and the vertuous Countesse your wife, such happy successe as your honours can desire, or I imagine.

  Your Lordships most duetifully
      to commaunde:
      ROBERT GREENE.

THE HISTORIE OF DORASTUS AND FAWNIA. Among al the passions wherewith humane mindes are perplexed, there is none that so galleth with restlesse despight, as the infectious soare of Iealousie: for all other griefes are eyther to bee appeased with sensible perswasions, to be cured with wholesome counsel, to be relieved in want, or by tract of time to be worne out, (Iealousie only excepted) which is so sawsed with suspitious doubtes, and pinching mistrust, that whoso seekes by friendly counsaile to rase out this hellish passion, it foorthwith suspected that he geveth this advise to cover his owne guiltinesse. Yea, who so is payned with this restlesse torment doubteth all, dystrusteth him-selfe, is alwayes frosen with feare, and fired with suspition, having that wherein consisteth all his joy to be the breeder of his miserie. Yea, it is such a heavy enemy to that holy estate of matrimony, sowing betweene the married couples such deadly seedes of secret hatred, as Love being once rased out by spightful distrust, there oft ensueth bloudy revenge, as this ensuing Hystorie manifestly prooveth: wherein Pandosto (furiously incensed by causelesse Iealousie) procured the death of his most loving and loyall wife, and his owne endlesse sorrow and misery. ❡ In the Countrey of Bohemia there raygned a King called Pandosto, whose fortunate successe in warres against his foes, and bountifull courtesie towardes his friendes in peace, made him to be greatly feared and loved of all men. This Pandosto had to Wife a Ladie called Bellaria, by birth royall, learned by education, faire by nature, by vertues famous, so that it was hard to judge whether her beautie, fortune, or vertue, wanne the greatest commendations. These two lincked together in perfect love, led their lives with such fortunate content, that their Subjects greatly rejoyced to see their quiet disposition. They had not beene married long, but Fortune (willing to increase their happines) lent them a sonne, so adorned with the gifts of nature, as the perfection of the Childe greatly augmented the love of the parentes, and the joys of their commons; in so much that the Bohemians, to shewe their inward joyes by outwarde actions,

5

made Bone-fires and triumphs throughout all the Kingdome, appointing Justes and Turneyes for the honour of their young Prince: whether resorted not onely his Nobles, but also divers Kings and Princes which were his neighbours, willing to shewe their friendship they ought to Pandosto, and to win fame and glory by their prowesse and valour. Pandosto, whose minde was fraught with princely liberality, entertayned the Kings, Princes, and noble men with such submisse curtesie and magnifical bounty, that they all sawe how willing he was to gratifie their good wils, making a feast for Subjects, which continued by the space of twentie dayes; all which time the Justes and Turneys were kept to the great content both of the Lordes and Ladies there present. This solemne tryumph being once ended, the assembly, taking their leave of Pandosto and Bellaria: the young sonne (who was called Garinter) was nursed up in the house to the great joy and content of the parents. ❡ Fortune envious of such happy successe, willing to shewe some signe of her inconstancie, turned her wheele, and darkned their bright sunne of prosperitie, with the mistie cloudes of mishap and misery. For it so happened that Egistus, King of Sycilia, who in his youth had bene brought up with Pandosto, desirous to shewe that neither tracte of time, nor distance of place could diminish their former friendship, provided a navie of ships, and sayled into Bohemia to visite his old friend and companion, who hearing of his arrivall, went himselfe in person, and his wife Bellaria, accompanied with a great traine of Lords and Ladies, to meete Egistus; and espying him, alighted from his horse, embraced him very lovingly protesting that nothing in the world could have happened more acceptable to him then his comming, wishing his wife to welcome his olde friend and acquaintance: who (to shewe how she liked him whom her husband loved) intertayned him with such familiar curtesie, as Egistus perceived himselfe to bee verie well welcome. After they had thus saluted and embraced eche other, they mounted againe on horsebacke and rode towards the Citie, devising and recounting, howe being children they had passed their youth in friendely

6

pastimes: where, by the meanes of the Citizens, Egistus was receyved with triumphs and showes in such sort, that he marvelled how on so small a warning they coulde make such preparation. ⁋ Passing the streetes thus with such rare sightes, they rode on to the Pallace, where Pandosto entertained Egistus and his Sycilians with such banqueting and sumptuous cheare, so royally, as they all had cause to commend his princely liberality; yea, the verie basest slave that was knowne to come from Sycilia was used with such curtesie, that Egistus might easily perceive how both hee and his were honored for his friendes sake. Bellaria (who in her time was the flower of curtesie), willing to show how unfaynedly shee looved her husband by his friends intertainement, used him likewise so familiarly that her countenance bewraied how her minde was affected towardes him: oftentimes comming her selfe into his bed chamber, to see that nothing should be amis to mislike him. This honest familiarity increased dayly more and more betwixt them; for Bellaria, noting in Egistus a princely and bountifull minde, adorned with sundrie and excellent qualities, and Egistus, finding in her a vertuous and curteous disposition, there grew such a secret uniting of their affections, that the one could not well be without the company of the other: in so much that when Pandosto was busied with such urgent affaires, that hee could not bee present with his friend Egistus, Bellaria would walke with him into the Garden, where they two in privat and pleasant devises would passe away the time to both their contents. This custome still continuing betwixt them, a certaine melancholy passion entring the minde of Pandosto drave him into sundry and doubtfull thoughts. First, he called to minde the beauty of his wife Bellaria, the comelines and braverie of his friend Egistus, thinking that Love was above all Lawes and therefore to be staid with no Law; that it was hard to put fire and flaxe together without burning; that their open pleasures might breede his secret displeasures. He considered with himselfe that Egistus was a man, and must needes love: that his wife was a woman, and therefore subject unto love,

7

and that where fancy forced, friendship was of no force. ¶ These and such like doubtfull thoughtes a long time smoothering in his stomacke, beganne at last to kindle in his minde a secret mistrust, which increased by suspition, grewe at last to be a flaming Iealousie, that so tormented him as he could take no rest. He then began to measure all their actions, and to misconstrue of their too private familiarite, judging that it was not for honest affection, but for disordinate fancy, so that hee began to watch them more narrowely to see if hee coulde gette any true or certaine proofe to confirme his doubtfull suspition. While thus he noted their lookes and gestures, and suspected their thoughtes and meaninges, they two seely soules who doubted nothing of this his treacherous intent, frequented daily eache others companie, which drave him into such a franticke passion, that he beganne to beare a secret hate to Egistus, and a lowring countenance to Bellaria, who marveiling at such unaccustomed frowns, began to cast beeyond the Moone, and to enter into a thousand sundrie thoughtes, which way she should offend her husband: but finding in her selfe a cleare conscience, ceassed to muse, until such time as she might find fit opportunitie to demaund the cause of his dumps. In the meane time Pandostoes minde was so farre charged with Iealously, that he did no longer doubt, but was assured (as he thought) that his Friend Egistus had entered a wrong pointe in his tables, and so had played him false play: wherupon desirous to revenge so great an injury, he thought best to dissemble the grudge with a faire and friendly countenance: and so under the shape of a friend, to shew him the tricke of a foe. Devising with himself a long time how he might best put away Egistus without suspition of treacherous murder, hee concluded at last to poyson him: which opinion pleasing his humour, he became resolute in his determination, and the better to bring the matter to passe he called unto him his cupbearer, with whom in secret he brake the matter: promising to him for the performance thereof to geve him a thousande crownes of yearely revenues: his cupbearer, eyther being of a good conscience, or willing for

8

fashion sake, to deny such a bloudy request, began with great reasons to perswade Pandosto from his determinate mischief: shewing him what an offence murther was to the Gods: how such unnaturall actions did more displease the heavens, than men, and that causelesse cruelty did seldome or never escape without revenge: he layd before his face, that Egistus was his friend, a King, and one that was come into his Kingdome, to confirme a league of perpetuall amitie betwixt them; that he had, and did shew him a most friendly countenance: how Egistus was not onely honoured of his owne people by obedience, but also loved of the Bohemians for his curtesie. And that if he now should, without any just or manifest cause, poyson him, it would not onely be a great dishonour to his Majestie, and a meanes to sow perpetuall enmity between the Sycilians and the Bohemians, but also his owne subjects would repine at such treacherous cruelty. These and such like perswasions of Franion (for so was his Cup-bearer called) could no whit prevaile to disswade him from his divillish enterprize: but remaining resolute in his determination (his fury so fired with rage, as it could not be appeased with reason) he began with bitter taunts to take up his man, and to lay before him two baites; preferment and death: saying that if he would poyson Egistus, he would advance him to high dignities: if he refused to doe it of an obstinate minde, no torture should be too great to requite his disobedience. Franion, seeing that to perswade Pandosto any more, was but to strive against the streame, consented, as soone as an opportunity would give him leave, to dispatch Egistus: wherewith Pandosto remained somewhat satisfied, hoping now he should be fully revenged of such mistrusted injuries, intending also as soon as Egistus was dead, to give his wife a sop of the same sawce, and so be rid of those which were the cause of his restles sorrow. While thus he lived in this hope, Franion being secret in his chamber, began to meditate with himselfe in these terms. ¶ Ah Franion, treason is loved of many, but the Traitor hated of all: unjust offences may for a time escape without danger, but never without revenge. Thou art servant to a King, and

9

must obey at command; yet Franion, against law and conscience, it is not good to resist a tyrant with armes, nor to please an unjust King with obedience. What shalt thou doe? Folly refused gold, and frenzie preferment: wisdome seeketh after dignity, and counsell keepeth for gaine. Egistus is a stranger to thee, and Pandosto thy Soveraigne: thou has little cause to respect the one, and oughtest to have great care to obèy the other. Thinke this Franion, that a pound of gold is worth a tunne of Lead, great gifts are little Gods: and preferment to a meane man is a whetstone to courage; there is nothing sweeter than promotion, nor lighter then report: care not then though most count thee a traitor, so all call thee rich. Dignity (Franion) advaunceth thy posteritie, and evil report can but hurt thy selfe. Know this, where Eagles builde, Falcons may prey; where Lyons haunt, Foxes may steale. Kings are knowne to commaund, servants are blamelesse to consent: feare not thou then to lift at Egistus, Pandosto shall beare the burthen. Yea but Franion, conscience is a worme that ever biteth, but never ceaseth: that which is rubbed with the stone Galactites will never bee hot. Flesh dipped in the Sea Ægeum will never bee sweete: the hearbe Trigion beeing once bit with an Aspis, never groweth, and conscience once stayned with innocent blood, is alwaies tyed to a guiltie remorse. Prefer thy content before riches, and a cleare minde before dignity; so beeing poore, thou shalt have rich peace, or else rich, thou shalt enjoy disquiet. ❡ Franion having muttered out these or such like words, seeing either he must die with a cleare minde, or live with a spotted conscience, he was so cumbred with divers cogitations that hee could take no rest: untill at last he determined to breake the matter to Egistus; but fearing that the King should eyther suspect or heare of such matters, he concealed the device till opportunitie would permit him to reveale it. Lingring thus in doubtfull feare, in an evening he went to Egistus lodging, and desirous to breake with him of certaine affaires that touched the King, after all were commaunded out of the Chamber, Franion made manifest the whole conspiracie which Pandosto had devised against him, desiring

10

Egistus not to account him a Traytor for bewraying his Maisters counsaile, but to thinke that he did it for conscience: hoping that although his Maister inflamed with rage, or incensed by some sinister reportes, or slanderous speeches, had imagined such causelesse mischiefe: yet when time should pacifie his anger, and try those talebearers but flattering Parasites, then he would count him as a faithfull Seruant that with such care had kept his Maisters credite. Egistus had not fully heard Franion tell forth his tale, but a quaking feare possessed all his limmes, thinking that there was some treason wrought, and that Franion did but shaddow his craft with these false colours: wherefore he began to waxe in choller, and saide that he doubted not Pandosto, sith he was his friend, and there had never as yet beene any breach of amity: he had not sought to invade his lands, to conspire with his enemies, to disswade his Subjects from their allegeance; but in word and thought he rested his at all times: he knew not therefore any cause that should moove Pandosto to seeke his death, but suspected it to be a compacted knavery of the Bohemians to bring the King and him to oddes. ¶ Franion staying him the middst of his talke, told him, that to dally with Princes was with the swannes to sing against their death, and that if the Bohemians had intended any such mischiefe, it might have beene better brought to passe then by revealing the conspiracie: therefore his Majesty did ill to misconstrue of his good meaning, sith his intent was to hinder treason, not to become a traytor; and to confirme his promises, if it pleased his Majestie to fly into Sicilia for the safegarde of his life, hee would goe with him, and if then he found not such a practise to be pretended, let his imagined treacherie be repayed with most monstrous torments. Egistus hearing the solemne protestation of Franion, beganne to consider, that in Love and Kingdomes, neither faith, nor lawe is to bee respected: doubting that Pandosto thought by his death to destroy his men, and with speedy warre to invade Sycilia. These and such doubtes throughly weyghed, he gave great thankes to Franion, promising if hee might with life returne to Syracusa, that hee would

11

create him a Duke in Sycilia: craving his Counsell how hee might escape out of the Countrie. Franion, who having some small skill in Navigation, was well acquainted with the Ports and havens, and knew every daunger in the Sea, joyning in counsell with the Maister of Egistus Navie, rigged all their ships, and setting them a flote, let them lie at anchor, to be in the more readines, when time and winde should serve. ❡ Fortune although blind, yet by chaunce favouring this just cause, sent them within six dayes a good gale of winde; which Franion seeing fit for their purpose, to put Pandosto out of suspition, the night before they should sayle, he went to him, and promised, that the next day he would put the device in practise, for he had got such a forcible poyson, as the very smell thereof wold procure suddain death. Pandosto was joyfull to heare this good newes, and thought every houre a day, till he might be glutted with bloudy revenge; but his suit had but ill successe. For Egistus fearing that delay might breede danger, and willing that the grass should not be cut from under his feete, taking bagge and baggage, by the helpe of Franion, conveied himselfe and his men out of a posterne gate of the Cittie, so secretly and speedily that without any suspition they got to the Sea shoare; where, with many a bitter curse taking their leave of Bohemia, they went aboord. Weighing their Anchors and hoisting sayle, they passed as fast as wind and sea would permit towards Sycilia: Egistus being a joyfull man that he had safely past such treacherous perils. But as they were quietly floating on the sea, so Pandosto and his Cittizens were in an oproare; for seeing that the Sycilians without taking their leave, were fled away by night, the Bohemians feared some treason, and the King thought that without question his suspition was true, seeing the Cup-bearer had bewrayed the sum of his secret pretence. Whereupon he began to imagine that Franion and his wife Bellaria had conspired with Egistus, and that the fervent affection shee bare him, was the onely meanes of his secret departure; in so much that incensed with rage, he commaunded that his wife should be carried straight to prison, untill they heard

12

further of his pleasure. The Guarde unwilling to lay their
hands one such a vertuous Princesse, and yet fearing the
Kings fury, went very sorrowfull to fulfill their charge:
comming to the Queenes lodging, they found her playing
with her yong sonne Garinter: unto whom with teares do-
ing the message, Bellaria astonished at such a hard censure,
and finding her cleere conscience a sure advocate to pleade
in her cause, went to the prison most willingly: where with
sighes and teares shee past away the time, till she might
come to her triall. ⟪ But Pandosto whose reason was suppressed with rage, and whose unbridled follie was incensed
with fury: seeing Franion had bewrayed his secrets, and
that Egistus might well be rayled on, but not revenged: determined to wreake all his wrath on poore Bellaria. He
therefore caused a generall proclamation to be made through
all his Realme, that the Queene and Egistus had by the helpe
of Franion, not onely committed most incestuous adultery,
but also had conspired the King's death; whereupon the
Traitor Franion was fled away with Egistus, and Bellaria
was most justly imprisoned. This proclamation being once
blazed through the country, although the vertuous disposition of the Queene did halfe discredit the contents, yet the
suddaine and speedy passage of Egistus, and the secret
departure of Franion, induced them (the circumstances
throughly considered) to thinke that both the proclamation
was true, and the King greatly injured: yet they pityed her
case, as sorrowful that so good a Lady should be crossed
with such adverse fortune. But the King, whose restlesse
rage would remit no pitty, thought that although he might
sufficiently requite his wives falshood with the bitter plague
of pinching penury, yet his minde should never be glutted
with revenge, till he might have fit time and opportunity to
repay the treachery of Egistus with a totall injury. But a
curst Cow hath oftentimes short hornes, and a willing minde
but a weake arme. For Pandosto although he felt that revenge was a spurre to warre, and that envy alwaies prof-
fereth steele, yet he saw, that Egistus was not onely of great
puissance and prowesse to withstand him, but had also many

13

Kings of his alliance to ayde him, if neede should serve: for he married the Emperours daughter of Russia. These and the like considerations something daunted Pandosto his courage, so that hee was content rather to put up a manifest injurie with peace, then hunt after revenge, dishonor and losse; determining since Egistus had escaped scot-free, that Bellaria should pay for all at an unreasonable price. ⟨ Remayning thus resolute in his determination, Bellaria continuing still in prison and hearing the contents of the Proclamation, knowing that her minde was never touched with such affection, nor that Egistus had ever offered her such discurtesie, would gladly have come to her answere, that both shee might have knowne her just accusers, and cleared her selfe of that guiltlesse crime. ⟨ But Pandosto was so inflamed with rage, and infected with Jelousie, as he would not vouchsafe to heare her, nor admit any just excuse; so that shee was faine to make a vertue of her neede and with patience to beare those heavie injuries. As thus shee lay crossed with calamities (a great cause to increase her griefe) she found her selfe quicke with childe: which as soone as she felt stirre in her body, she burst forth into bitter teares, exclayming against fortune in these termes. ⟨ Alas, Bellaria, how infortunate art thou, because fortunate: Better thou hadst beene borne a beggar, then a Prince, so shouldest thou have bridled Fortune with want, where now shee sporteth her selfe with thy plentie. Ah happy life, where poore thoughts, and meane desires live in secure content, not fearing Fortune because too low for Fortune. Thou seest now, Bellaria that care is a companion to honor, not to povertie; that high Cedars are crushed with tempests, when low shrubs are not touched with the winde; pretious Diamonds are cut with the file, when despised pibbles lye safe in the sand. Delphos is sought to by Princes, not beggers: and Fortunes Altars smoke with kings presents, not with poore mens gifts. Happie are such Bellaria, that curse Fortune for contempt, not feare: and may wish they were, not sorrow they have beene. Thou art a Princesse Bellaria, and yet a prisoner; borne to the one by descent, assigned to the other by dispite:

14

accused without cause, and therefore oughtest to dye without care: for patience is a shield against Fortune, and a
guiltlesse minde yeeldeth not to sorrow. Ah but infamy
galleth unto death, and liveth after death: Report is plumed
with times feathers, and Envie oftentimes soundeth Fames
trumpet: the suspected adultery shall fly in the ayre, and
thy knowne vertues shall lye hid in the Earth; one Moale
staineth a whole Face: and what is once spotted with infamy can hardly be worne out with time. Die then Bellaria, Bellaria die: for if the Gods should say thou art guiltlesse, yet envie would heare the Gods, but never beleeve
the Gods. Ah haplesse wretch, cease these tearmes: desperate thoughtes are fit for them that feare shame, not for such
as hope for credite. Pandosto hath darkened thy fame, but
shall never discredite thy vertues. Suspition may enter a
false action, but proofe shall never put in his plea: care not
then for envie, sith report hath a blister on her tongue: and
let sorrow baite them which offend, not touch thee that art
faultlesse. But alas poore soule, how canst thou but sorrow? Thou art with childe, and by him, that in steed of
kind pittie, pincheth thee in cold prison. ⁋ And with that,
such gasping sighes so stopping her breath, that shee could
not utter more words, but wringing her hands, and gushing
forth streames of teares, shee passed away the time with
bitter complaints. The Jaylor pitying those her heavie passions, thinking that if the King knew she were with childe,
he would somewhat appease his fury and release her from
prison, went in al hast, and certified Pandosto, what the
effect of Bellarias complaint was; who no sooner heard the
Jailor say she was with childe, but as one possessed with a
phranzie, he rose up in a rage, swearing that shee and the
basterd brat she was [big] withall should die, if the Gods
themselves said no; thinking that surely by computation of
time, that Egistus and not he was father to the childe. This
suspitious thought galled a fresh this halfe healed sore, in
so much as he could take no rest, untill he might mittigate
his choller with a just revenge, which happened presently
after. For Bellaria was brought to bed of a faire and

15

beautifull daughter: which no sooner Pandosto hearde, but he determined that both Bellaria and the young infant should be burnt with fire. His Nobles, hearing of the kings cruell sentence, sought by perswasions to divert him from his bloodie determination: laying before his face the innocencie of the childe, and vertuous disposition of his wife, how she had continually loved and honoured him so tenderly, that without due proofe he could not, nor ought not to appeach her of that crime. And if she had faulted, yet it were more honourable to pardon with mercy, then to punish with extremity, and more kingly, to be commended of pitty, than accused of rigour: and as for the childe, if he should punish it for the mothers offence, it were to strive against nature and justice; and that unnatural actions doe more offend the Gods then men: how causelesse cruelty, nor innocent blood never scapes without revenge. These and such like reasons could not appease his rage, but he rested resolute in this, that Bellaria beeing an Adultresse, the childe was a Bastard, and he would not suffer that such an infamous brat should call him Father. Yet at last (seeing his Noble men were importunate upon him) he was content to spare the childes life, and yet to put it to a worse death. For he found out this devise, that seeing (as he thought) it came by fortune, so he would commit it to the charge of Fortune, and therefore caused a little cock-boat to be provided, wherein he meant to put the babe, and then send it to the mercies of the Seas and the destenies. From this his Peeres in no wise could perswade him, but that he sent presently two of his guard to fetch the childe: who being come to the prison, and with weeping teares recounting their Maisters message: Bellaria no sooner heard the rigorious resolution of her mercilesse husband, but she fell downe in a swound, so that all thought she had bin dead: yet at last being come to her selfe, shee cryed and screeched out in this wise. ❡ Alas sweete infortunate babe, scarce borne, before envied by fortune, would the day of thy birth had beene the terme of thy life: then shouldest thou have made an ende to care and prevented thy Fathers rigour. Thy faults cannot yet deserve such hatefull

16

revenge, thy dayes are too short for so sharpe a doome, but thy untimely death must pay thy Mothers Debts, and her guiltlesse crime must bee thy gastly curse. And shalt thou, sweete babe be committed to Fortune, when thou art already spited by Fortune? Shall the Seas be thy harbour, and the hard boate thy cradle? Shall thy tender Mouth, in steede of sweete kisses, be nipped with bitter stormes? Shalt thou have the whistling windes for thy Lullabie, and the salt Sea fome in steede of sweete milke? Alas, what destinies would assigne such hard hap? What Father would be so cruell? or what Gods will not revenge such rigor? Let me kisse thy lippes (sweete Infant) and wet thy tender cheekes with my teares, and put this chayne about thy necke, that if fortune save thee, it may helpe to succour thee. This, since thou must goe to surge in the gastfull Seas, with a sorrowfull kisse I bid thee farewell, and I pray the Gods thou maist fare well. ⁊ Such, and so great was her griefe, that her vitall spirits being suppressed with sorrow, she fell againe downe into a trance, having her sences so sotted with care, that after she was revived yet shee lost her memorie, and lay for a great time without moving, as one in a trance. The guard left her in this perplexitie, and carried the child to the King, who quite devoide of pity commanded that without delay it should bee put in the boat, having neither saile nor rudder to guid it, and so to bee carried into the midst of the sea, and there left to the wind and wave as the destinies please to appoint. The very shipmen, seeing the sweete countenance of the yong babe, began to accuse the King of rigor, and to pity the childs hard fortune: but feare constrayned them to that which their nature did abhorre; so that they placed it in one of the ends of the boat, and with a few green bows made a homely cabben to shrowd it as they could from wind and weather: having thus trimmed the boat they tied it to a ship, and so haled it into the mayne Sea, and then cut in sunder the coarde, which they had no sooner done, but there arose a mighty tempest, which tossed the little Boate so vehemently in the waves, that the shipmen thought it could not long continue without sincking, yea the storme grewe so great, that with much labour and perill they got to the shoare. ⦅ But leaving the Childe to her fortunes. Againe to Pandosto, who not yet glutted with sufficient revenge, devised which way he should best increase his Wives calamitie. But first assembling his Nobles and Counsellors, hee called her for the more reproch into open Court, where it was objected against her, that she had committed adulterie with Egistus, and conspired with Franion to poyson Pandosto her husband, but their pretence being partely spyed, she counselled them to flie away by night for their better safety. Bellaria, who standing like a prisoner at the Barre, feeling in her selfe a cleare Conscience to withstand her false accusers: seeing that no lesse then death could pacifie her husbands wrath, waxed bolde, and desired that she might have Lawe and Justice, for mercy shee neyther craved nor hoped for; and that those perjured wretches, which had falsely accused her to the King, might be brought before her face, to give in evidence. But Pandosto, whose rage and Jealousie was such, no reason, nor equitie could appease: tolde her, that for her accusers they were of such credite, as their wordes were sufficient witnesse, and that the sodaine and secret flight of Egistus and Franion confirmed that which they had confessed: and as for her, it was her parte to deny such a monstrus crime, and to be impudent in forswearing the fact, since shee had past all shame in committing the fault; but her stale countenance should stand for no coyne, for as the Bastard which she bare was served, so she should with some cruell death be requited. Bellaria no whit dismayed with this rough reply, tolde her Husband Pandosto, that he spake upon choller, and not conscience: for her vertuous life had beene ever such, as no spot of suspition could ever staine. And if she had borne a friendly countenaunce to Egistus, it was in respect he was his friende, and not for any lusting affection: therefore if she were condemned without any further proofe, it was rigour, and not Law. ⦅ The noble men which sate in judgement, said that Bellaria spake reason, and intreated the king that the accusers might be openly examined, and sworne, and if then the

18

evidence were such, as the Jury might finde her guilty (for seeing she was a Prince she ought to be tryed by her peeres) then let her have such punishment as the extremitie of the Law will assigne to such malefactors. The king presently made answere, that in this case he might, and would dispence with the Law, and that the Jury being once panneld, they should take his word for sufficient evidence, otherwise he would make the proudest of them repent it. The noble men seeing the king in choler were all whist, but Bellaria, whose life then hung in the ballaunce, fearing more perpetuall infamie then momentarie death, tolde the king, if his furie might stand for a Law that it were vaine to have the Jury yeeld their verdit; and therefore she fell downe upon her knees, and desired the king that for the love he bare to his young sonne Garinter, whome she brought into the world, that hee woulde graunt her a request, which was this, that it would please his majestie to send sixe of his noble men whome he best trusted, to the Isle of Delphos, there to enquire of the Oracle of Apollo, whether she had committed adultery with Egistus, or conspired to poyson with Franion: and if the God Apollo, who by his devine essence knew al secrets, gave answere that she was guiltie, she were content to suffer any torment, were it never so terrible. The request was so reasonable, that Pandosto could not for shame deny it, unlesse he would bee counted of all his subjects more wilfull then wise, he therefore agreed, that with as much speede as might be there should be certaine Embassadores dispatched to the Ile of Delphos; and in the meane season he commanded that his wife should be kept in close prison.
❡ Bellaria having obtained this graunt was now more carefull for her little babe that floated on the Seas, then sorrowful for her owne mishap. For of that she doubted: of her selfe shee was assured, knowing if Apollo should give Oracle according to the thoughts of the hart, yet the sentence should goe one her side, such was the clearenes of her minde in this case. But Pandosto (whose suspitious heade still remained in one song) chose out sixe of his Nobility, whom hee knew were scarse indifferent men in the Queenes behalfe,

19

and providing all things fit for their journey, sent them to
Delphos: they willing to fulfill the Kinges commaund, and
desirous to see the situation and custome of the Iland, dispatched their affaires with as much speede as might be, and
embarked themselves to this voyage, which (the wind and
weather serving fit for their purpose) was soone ended.
For within three weekes they arrived at Delphos, where
they were no sooner set on lande, but with great devotion
they went to the Temple of Apollo, and there offring sacrifice to the God, and giftes to the Priest, as the custome was,
they humbly craved an aunswere of their demaund: they
had not long kneeled at the Altar, but Apollo with a loude
voice saide: Bohemians, what you finde behinde the Alter
take and depart. They forthwith obeying the Oracle founde
a scroule of parchment, wherein was written these words
in letters of Golde, —

THE ORACLE.

SUSPITION IS NO PROOFE: JEALOUSIE IS AN UNEQUALL
JUDGE: BELLARIA IS CHAST; EGISTUS BLAMELESSE:
FRANION A TRUE SUBJECT; PANDOSTO TREACHEROUS:
HIS BABE AN INNOCENT, AND THE KING SHAL LIVE WITH-
OUT AN HEIRE: IF THAT WHICH IS LOST BE NOT FOUNDE.

❡ As soone as they had taken out this scroule, the Priest of
the God commaunded them that they should not presume
to read it, before they came in the presence of Pandosto:
unlesse they would incurre the displeasure of Apollo. The
Bohemian Lords carefully obeying his commaund, taking
their leave of the Priest, with great reverence departed out
of the Temple, and went to their ships, and assoone as wind
would permit them, sailed toward Bohemia, whither in short
time they safely arrived, and with great tryumph issuing
out of their Ships went to the Kinges pallace, whom they
found in his chamber accompanied with other Noble men:
Pandosto no sooner saw them, but with a merrie countenaunce he welcomed them home, asking what newes: they
told his Majestie that they had received an aunswere of the
God written in a scroule, but with this charge, that they

should not read the contents before they came in the presence of the King, and with that they delivered him the parchment: but his Noble men entreated him that sith therein was contayned either the safetie of his Wives life, and honesty, or her death, and perpetuall infamy, that he would have his Nobles and Commons assembled in the judgement Hall, where the Queene brought in as prysoner, should heare the contents: if shee were found guilty by the Oracle of the God, then all should have cause to thinke his rigour proceeded of due desert: if her Grace were found faultlesse, then shee should bee cleared before all, sith she had bene accused openly. This pleased the King so, that he appointed the day, and assembled al his Lords and Commons, and caused the Queene to be brought in before the judgement seat, commaunding that the inditement shoulde bee read, wherein she was accused of adultery with Egistus, and of conspiracy with Franion: Bellaria hearing the contentes, was no whit astonished, but made this chearefull aunswer: ❡ If the devine powers bee privy to humane actions (as no doubt they are) I hope my patience shall make fortune blushe, and my unspotted life shall staine spightful discredit. For although lying Report hath sought to appeach mine honor, and Suspition hath intended to soyle my credit with infamie: yet where Vertue keepeth the Forte, Report and suspition may assayle, but never sack: how I have led my life before Egistus comming, I appeale Pandosto to the Gods and to thy -conscience. What hath past betwixt him and me, the Gods only know, and I hope will presently reveale: that I loved Egistus I can not denie: that I honored him I shame not to confesse: to the one I was forced by his vertues, to the other for his dignities. But as touching lascivious lust, I say Egistus is honest, and hope my selfe to be found without spot: for Franion, I can neither accuse him nor excuse him, for I was not privie to his departure, and that this is true which I have heere rehearsed, I referre myself to the devine Oracle. ❡ Bellaria had no sooner sayd, but the King commaunded that one of his Dukes should read the contentes of the scroule; which after the commons had heard, they gave a great showt,

21

rejoysing and clapping their hands that the Queene was cleare of that false accusation: but the king whose conscience was a witnesse against him of his witlesse furie, and false suspected Iealousie, was so ashamed of his rashe folly, that he entreated his nobles to perswade Bellaria to forgive and forget these injuries: promising not onely to shew himselfe a loyall and loving husband, but also to reconcile himselfe to Egistus, and Franion: revealing then before them all the cause of their secrete flighte, and how treacherously hee thought to have practised his death, if the good minde of his Cupbearer had not prevented his purpose. As thus he was relating the whole matter, there was worde brought him that his young sonne Garinter was sodainly dead, which newes so soone as Bellaria heard, surcharged before with extreame joy, and now suppressed with heavie sorrowe, her vital spirites were so stopped, that she fell downe presently dead, and could never be revived. This sodaine sight so appalled the Kings Sences, that he sancke from his seat in a sound, so as he was fayne to be carried by his nobles to his Pallace, where hee lay by the space of three dayes without speech: his commons were as men in dispaire, so diversely distressed: there was nothing but mourning and lamentation to be heard throughout al Bohemia: their young Prince dead, their vertuous Queene bereaved of her life, and their King and Soveraigne in great hazard: this tragicall discourse of fortune so daunted them, as they went like shadowes, not men; yet somewhat to comfort their heavie hearts, they heard that Pandosto was come to himselfe, and had recovered his speache, who as in a fury brayed out these bitter speaches: ❡ O miserable Pandosto, what surer witnesse then conscience? what thoughts more sower then suspition? What plague more bad then Iealousie? Unnaturall actions offend the Gods more than men, and causelesse crueltie never scapes without revenge: I have committed such a bloudy fact, as repent I may, but recall I cannot. Ah Iealousie, a hell to the minde, and a horror to the conscience, suppressing reason, and inciting rage; a worse passion then phrensie, a greater plague than madnesse. Are the Gods

22

just? Then let them revenge such brutishe crueltie: my innocent Babe I have drowned in the Seas; my loving wife I have slaine with slaunderous suspition; my trusty friend I have sought to betray, and yet the Gods are slacke to plague such offences. Ah unjust Apollo, Pandosto is the man that hath committed the faulte: why should Garinter, seely childe, abide the paine? Well sith the Gods meane to prolong my dayes, to increase my dolour, I will offer my guiltie bloud a sacrifice to those sackles soules, whose lives are lost by my rigorous folly. ¶ And with that he reached at a Rapier, to have murdered himselfe, but his Peeres being present, stayed him from such a bloudy acte: perswading him to think, that the Commonwealth consisted on his safetie, and that those sheep could not but perish, that wanted a sheepheard: wishing that if hee would not live for himselfe, yet he should have care of his subjects, and to put such fancies out of his minde, sith in sores past help, salves do not heale, but hurt: and in things past cure, care is a corrosive: with these and such like perswasions the Kinge was overcome, and began somewhat to quiet his minde: so that assoone as he could goe abroad, hee caused his wife to be embalmed, and wrapt in lead with her young sonne Garinter; erecting a rich and famous Sepulchre, wherein hee intombed them both, making such solemn obsequies at her funeral, as al Bohemia might perceive he did greatly repent him of his forepassed folly: causing this Epitaph to be ingraven on her Tombe in letters of Gold:

¶ THE EPITAPH.

HERE LYES ENTOMBDE BELLARIA FAIRE,
FALSLY ACCUSED TO BE UNCHASTE:
CLEARED BY APOLLOS SACRED DOOME,
YET SLAINE BY JEALOUSIE AT LAST.

WHAT ERE THOU BE THAT PASSEST BY,
CURSSE HIM, THAT CAUSDE THIS QUEENE TO DIE.

¶ This epitaph being ingraven, Pandosto would once a day repaire to the Tombe, and there with watry plaintes bewaile his misfortune; coveting no other companion but sorrowe, nor

23

no other harmonie, but repentance. But leaving him to his dolorous passions, at last let us come to shewe the tragicall discourse of the young infant. ❡ Who beeing tossed with Winde and Wave, floated two whole daies without succour, readie at every puffe to bee drowned in the Sea, till at last the Tempest ceassed and the little boate was driven with the tyde into the Coast of Sycilia, where sticking uppon the sandes it rested. Fortune minding to be wanton, willing to shewe that as she hath wrinckles on her browes: so shee hath dimples in her cheekes; thought after so many sower lookes, to lend a fayned smile, and after a puffing storme, to bring a pretty calme: shee began 'thus to dally. It fortuned a poore mercenary Sheepheard, that dwelled in Sycilia, who got his living by other mens flockes, missed one of his sheepe, and thinking it had strayed into the covert, that was hard by, sought very diligently to find that which he could not see, fearing either that the Wolves or Eagles had undone him (for hee was so poore, as a sheepe was halfe his substaunce), wandered downe toward the Sea cliffes, to see if perchaunce the sheepe was browsing on the sea Ivy, whereon they greatly doe feede, but not finding her there, as he was ready to returne to his flocke, hee heard a child crie: but knowing there was no house nere, he thought he had mistaken the sound, and that it was the bleatyng of his Sheepe. Wherefore looking more narrowely, as he cast his eye to the Sea, he spyed a little boate, from whence as he attentively listened, he might heare the cry to come: standing a good while in a maze, at last he went to the shoare, and wading to the boate, as he looked in, he saw the little babe lying al alone, ready to die for hunger and colde, wrapped in a Mantle of Scarlet, richley imbrodered with Golde, and having a chayne about the necke. ❡ The Sheepeheard, who before had never seene so faire a Babe, nor so riche Iewels, thought assuredly, that it was some little God, and began with great devocion to knock on his breast. The Babe, who wrythed with the head, to seeke for the pap, began againe to cry a fresh, whereby the poore man knew that it was a Childe, which by some sinister meanes was

24

driven thither by distresse of weather; marvailing how such a seely infant, which by the Mantle, and the Chayne, could not be but borne of Noble Parentage, should be so hardly crossed with deadly mishap. The poore sheepheard perplexed thus with divers thoughts, tooke pitty of the childe, and determined with himselfe to carry it to the King, that there it might be brought up, according to the worthinesse of birth; for his ability coulde not afforde to foster it, though his good minde was willing to further it. Taking therefore the Chylde in his armes, as he foulded the mantle together, the better to defend it from colde, there fell downe at his foote a very faire and riche purse, wherein he founde a great summe of golde: which sight so revived the shepheards spirits, as he was greatly ravished with joy, and daunted with feare; Ioyfull to see such a summe in his power, and fearefull if it should be knowne, that it might breede his further daunger. Necessitie wisht him at least, to retaine the Golde, though he would not keepe the childe: the simplicity of his conscience scared him from such deceiptfull briberie. Thus was the poore manne perplexed with a doubtfull Dilemma, until at last the covetousnesse of the coyne overcame him: for what will not the greedy desire of Golde cause a man to doe? So that he was resolved in himselfe to foster the child, and with the summe to relieve his want: resting thus resolute in this point he left seeking of his sheepe, and as covertly, and secretly as he coulde, went by a by way to his house, least any of his neighbours should perceave his carriage: as soone as he was got home, entring in at the doore, the childe began to crie, which his wife hearing, and seeing her husband with a yong babe in his armes, began to bee somewhat jelousse, yet marveiling that her husband should be so wanton abroad, sith he was so quiet at home: but as women are naturally given to beleeve the worste, so his wife thinking it was some bastard: beganne to crowe against her goodman, and taking up a cudgel (for the most maister went breechles) sware solemnly that shee would make clubs trumps, if hee brought any bastard brat within her dores. The goodman, seeing his wife in her majestie

25

with her mace in her hand, thought it was time to bowe for feare of blowes, and desired her to be quiet, for there was non such matter; but if she could holde her peace, they were made for ever: and with that he told her the whole matter, how he had found the childe in a little boat, without any succour, wrapped in that costly mantle, and having that rich chaine about the neck: but at last when he shewed her the purse full of gold, she began to simper something sweetely, and taking her husband about the neck, kissed him after her homely fashion: saying that she hoped God had seene their want, and now ment to relieeve their poverty, and seeing they could get no children, had sent them this little babe to be their heire. Take heede in any case (quoth the shepherd) that you be secret, and blabbe it not out when you meete with your gossippes, for if you doe, we are like not only to loose the Golde and Iewels, but our other goodes and lives. Tush (quoth his wife), profit is a good hatch before the doore: feare not, I have other things to talke of then of this; but I pray you let us lay up the money surely, and the Iewels, least by any mishap it be spied. ¶ After that they had set all things in order, the shepheard went to his sheepe with a merry note, and the good wife learned to sing lullaby at home with her yong babe, wrapping it in a homely blanket in sted of a rich mantle; nourishing it so clenly and carefully as it began to bee a jolly girle, in so much that they began both of them to be very fond of it, seeing, as it waxed in age, so it increased in beauty. The shepheard every night at his comming home, would sing and daunce it on his knee, and prattle, that in a short time it began to speake, and call him Dad, and her Mam: at last when it grew to ripe yeeres, that it was about seven yeares old, the shepheard left keeping of other mens sheepe, and with the money he found in the purse, he bought him the lease of a pretty farme, and got a smal flocke of sheepe, which when Fawnia (for so they named the child) came to the age of ten yeres, hee set her to keepe, and shee with such diligence performed her charge as the sheepe prospered marveilously under her hand. Fawnia thought Porrus had been her father, and

26

Mopsa her mother, (for so was the shepheard and his wife called) honoured and obeyed them with such reverence, that all the neighbours praised the duetifull obedience of the child. Porrus grewe in a short time to bee a man of some wealth, and credite; for fortune so favoured him in having no charge but Fawnia, that he began to purchase land, intending after his death to give it to his daughter; so that diverse rich farmers sonnes came as woers to his house: for Fawnia was something clenly attired, beeing of such singular beautie and excellent witte, that whoso sawe her, would have thought shee had bene some heavenly nymph, and not a mortal creature: in so much, that when she came to the age of sixteene yeeres, shee so increased with exquisite perfection both of body and minde, as her natural disposition did bewray that she was borne of some high parentage; but the people thinking she was daughter to the shephard Porrus, rested only amazed at hir beauty and wit; yea she won such favour and commendations in every mans eye, as her beautie was not only praysed in the countrey, but also spoken of in the Court: yet such was her submisse modestie, that although her praise daily increased, her mind was no whit puffed up with pride, but humbled her selfe as became a country mayde and the daughter of a poore sheepheard. Every day she went forth with her sheepe to the field, keeping them with such care and diligence, as al men thought she was verie painfull, defending her face from the heat of the sunne with no other vale, but with a garland made of bowes and flowers; which attire became her so gallantly, as shee seemed to bee the Goddesse Flora her selfe for beauty. ❡ Fortune, who al this while had shewed a frendly face, began now to turne her back, and to shewe a lowring countenance, intending as she had given Fawnia a slender checke, so she would give her a harder mate: to bring which to passe, she layd her traine on this wise. Egistus had but one only son called Dorastus, about the age of twenty yeeres; a prince so decked and adorned with the gifts of nature: so fraught with beauty and vertuous qualities, as not onely his father joyed to have so

27

good a sonne, and al his commons rejoyced that God had lent them such a noble Prince to succeede in the Kingdom. Egistus placing al his joy in the perfection of his sonne: seeing that he was now mariage-able, sent Embassadors to the king of Denmarke, to intreate a mariage betweene him and his daughter, who willingly consenting, made answer, that the next spring, if it please Egistus with his sonne to come into Denmarke, hee doubted not but they should agree upon reasonable conditions. Egistus resting satisfied with this friendly answer, thought convenient in the meane time to breake with his sonne: finding therefore on a day fit opportunity, he spake to him in these fatherly tearmes: ❡ Dorastus, thy youth warneth me to prevent the worst, and mine age to provide the best. Oportunities neglected, are signes of folly: actions measured by time, are seldome bitten with repentance: thou art young, and I olde: age hath taught me that, which thy youth cannot yet conceive. I therefore will counsell thee as a father, hoping thou wilt obey as a childe. Thou seest my white hayres are blossomes for the grave, and thy freshe colour fruite for time and fortune, so that it behooveth me to thinke how to dye, and for thee to care how to live. My crowne I must leave by death, and thou enjoy my Kingdome by succession, wherein I hope thy vertue and prowesse shall bee such, as though my subjectes want my person, yet they shall see in thee my perfection. That nothing either may faile to satisfie thy minde, or increase thy dignities: the onely care I have is to see thee well marryed before I die, and thou become olde. ❡ Dorastus, who from his infancy, delighted rather to die with Mars in the Fielde then to dally with Venus in the Chamber, fearing to displease his father, and yet not willing to be wed, made him this reuerent answere. ❡ Sir, there is no greater bond then duetie, nor no straiter law then nature: disobedience in youth is often galled with despight in age. The commaund of the father ought to be a constraint to the childe: so parentes willes are laws, so they passe not all laws: may it please your Grace therefore to appoint whome I shall love, rather then by deniall I should be appeached of disobedience:

I rest content to love, though it bee the only thing I hate. ¶ Egistus hearing his sonne to flie so farre from the marke, began to be somewhat chollericke, and therefore made him this hastie aunswere. ¶ What Dorastus canst thou not love? Commeth this cynicall passion of prone desires or peevish frowardnesse? What durst thou thinke thy selfe to good for all, or none good inough for thee? I tell thee, Dorastus, there is nothing sweeter then youth, nor swifter decreasing while it is increasing. Time past with folly may bee repented, but not recalled. If thou marrie in age, thy wives freshe couloures will breede in thee dead thoughtes and suspition, and thy white hayres her lothesomenesse and sorrowe. For Venus affections are not fed with King-domes, or treasures, but with youthfull conceits and sweet amours. Vulcan was allotted to shake the tree, but Mars allowed to reape the fruite. Yeelde Dorastus to thy Fathers perswasions, which may prevent thy perils. I have chosen thee a Wife, faire by nature, royall by birth, by vertues famous, learned by education and rich by possessions, so that it is hard to judge whether her bounty, or fortune, her beauty, or vertue bee of greater force: I mean, Dorastus, Euphrania daughter and heire to the King of Denmarke. ¶ Egistus pausing here a while, looking when his son should make him answere, and seeing that he stoode still as one in a trance, he shooke him up thus sharply. ¶ Well Dorastus take heede, the tree Alpya wasteth not with fire, but with-ereth with the dewe: that which love nourisheth not, per-isheth with hate: if thou like Euphrania, thou breedest my content, and in loving her thou shalt have my love, other-wise; and with that hee flung from his sonne in a rage, leav-ing him a sorrowfull man, in that he had by deniall dis-pleased his Father, and halfe angrie with him selfe that hee could not yeelde to that passion, whereto both reason and his Father perswaded him: but see how fortune is plumed with times feathers, and how shee can minister strange causes to breede straunge effects. ¶ It happened not long after this that there was a meeting of all the Farmers Daugh-ters in Sycilia, whither Fawnia was also bidden as the

29

mistres of the feast, who having attired her selfe in her best garments, went among the rest of her companions to the merry meeting: there spending the day in such homely pastimes as shepheards use. As the evening grew on, and their sportes ceased, ech taking their leave at other, Fawnia desiring one of her companions to beare her companie, went home by the flocke, to see if they were well folded, and as they returned, it fortuned that Dorastus (who all that daye had bene hawking, and kilde store of game) incountred by the way these two mayds, and casting his eye sodenly on Fawnia, he was halfe afraid, fearing that with Acteon he had seene Diana: for hee thought such exquisite perfection could not be founde in any mortall creature. As thus he stoode in a maze, one of his Pages told him, that the maide with the garland on her heade was Fawnia, the faire shepheard, whose beauty was so much talked of in the Court. Dorastus desirous to see if nature had adorned her minde with any inward qualities, as she had decked her body with outward shape, began to question with her whose daughter she was, of what age and how she had bin trained up, who answered him with such modest reverence and sharpnesse of witte, that Dorastus thought her outward beautie was but a counterfait to darken her inward qualities, wondring how so courtly behaviour could be found in so simple a cottage, and cursing fortune that had shadowed wit and beauty with such hard fortune. As thus he held her a long while with chat, Beauty seeing him at discovert, thought not to lose the vantage, but strooke him so deeply with an invenomed shafte, as he wholy lost his libertie, and became a slave to Love, which before contemned love, glad now to gaze on a poore shepheard, who before refused the offer of a riche Princesse; for the perfection of Fawnia had so fired his fancie as he felt his minde greatly chaunged, and his affections altered, cursing Love that had wrought such a chaunge, and blaming the basenesse of his mind, that would make such a choice: but thinking these were but passionat toies that might be thrust out at pleasure, to avoid the Syren that inchaunted him, he put spurs to his horse, and bad this

30

faire shepheard farewell. ❡ Fawnia (who all this while had marked the princely gesture of Dorastus) seeing his face so welfeatured, and each lim so perfectly framed, began greatly to praise his perfection, commending him so long, till she found her selfe faultie, and perceived that if she waded but a little further, she might slippe over her shooes: shee therefore seeking to quench that fire which never was put out, went home, and faining her selfe not well at ease, got her to bed: where casting a thousand thoughts in her head, she could take no rest: for if she waked, she began to call to minde his beautie, and thinking to beguile such thoughts with sleepe, she then dreamed of his perfection: pestered thus with these unacquainted passions, she passed the night as she could in short slumbers. ❡ Dorastus (who all this while rode with a flea in his eare) could not by any meanes forget the sweete favour of Fawnia, but rested so bewitched with her wit and beauty, as hee could take no rest. He felt fancy to give the assault, and his wounded mind readie to yeeld as van-quished: yet he began with divers considerations to sup-presse this frantick affection, calling to minde, that Fawnia was a shepheard, one not worthy to bee looked at of a Prince, much less to bee loved of such a potentate, thinking what a discredite it were to himself, and what a griefe it would be to his father, blaming fortune and accusing his owne follie, that should bee so fond as but once to cast a glaunce at such a country slut. As thus he was raging against him selfe, Love fearing if shee dallied long, to loose her champion, stept more nigh, and gave him such a fresh wounde as it pearst him at the heart, that he was faine to yeeld, maugre his face, and to forsake the companie and gette him to his chamber: where being solemnly set, hee burst into these passionate tearmes. ❡ Ah, Dorastus, art thou alone? No not alone, while thou art tired with these unacquainted passions. Yeld to fancy, thou canst not by thy fathers counsaile, but in a frenzie thou art by just desti-nies. Thy father were content, if thou couldest love, and thou therefore discontent, because thou doest love. O de-vine Love, feared of men because honoured of the Gods,

31

not to be suppressed by wisdome, because not to be comprehended by reason: without Lawe, and therefore above all Law. How now Dorastus, why doest thou blaze that with praises, which thou hast cause to blaspheme without curses? yet why should they curse Love that are in Love? Blush Dorastus at thy fortune, thy choice, thy love: thy thoughts cannot be uttered without shame, nor thy affections without discredit. Ah Fawnia, sweete Fawnia, thy beautie Fawnia. Shamest not thou Dorastus to name one unfitte for thy birth, thy dignities, thy Kingdomes? Dye Dorastus, Dorastus die. Better hadst thou perish with high desires, then live in base thoughts. Yea but, beautie must be obeyed, because it is beauty, yet framed of the Gods to feede the eye, not to fetter the heart. Ah but he that striveth against Love, shooteth with them of Scyrum against the wind, and with the Cockeatrice pecketh against the steele. I will therefore obey, because I must obey. Fawnia, yea Fawnia shall be my fortune, in spight of fortune. The Gods above disdain not to love women beneath. Phœbus liked Sibilla, Jupiter Io, and why not I then Fawnia? one something inferiour to these in birth, but farre superiour to them in beautie, borne to be a Shepheard, but worthy to be a Goddesse. Ah Dorastus, wilt thou so forget thy selfe as to suffer affection to suppresse wisedome, and Love to violate thine honour? How sower will thy choice be to thy Father, sorrowfull to thy Subjects, to thy friends a griefe, most gladsome to thy foes! Subdue then thy affections, and cease to love her whome thou couldst not love, unlesse blinded with too much love. Tushe I talke to the wind, and in seeking to prevent the causes, I further the effectes. I will yet praise Fawnia; honour, yea and love Fawnia, and at this day followe content, not counsaile. Doo Dorastus, thou canst but repent: and with that his Page came into the chamber, whereupon hee ceased from his complaints, hoping that time would weare out that which fortune had wrought. As thus he was pained, so poore Fawnia was diversely perplexed: for the next morning getting up very earely, she went to her sheepe, thinking with hard labours to passe away her new conceived amours, beginning very busily to drive them to the field, and then to shifte the foldes, at last (wearied with toile) she sate her down, where (poore soule) she was more tryed with fond affections: for love beganne to assault her, in so much that as she sate upon the side of a hill, she began to accuse her owne folly in these tearmes. ⁋ Infortunate Fawnia, and therefore infortunate because Fawnia, thy shepherds hooke sheweth thy poore state, thy proud desires an aspiring mind: the one declareth thy want, the other thy pride. No bastard hauke must soare so high as the Hobbie, no Fowle gaze against the Sunne but the Eagle, actions wrought against nature reape despight, and thoughts above Fortune disdaine. Fawnia, thou art a shepheard, daughter to poore Porrus: if thou rest content with this, thou art like to stande, if thou climbe thou art sure to fal. The Herb Anita growing higher then sixe ynches becommeth a weede. Nylus flowing more then twelve cubits procureth a dearth. Daring affections that passe measure, are cut shorte by time or fortune: suppresse then Fawnia those thoughts which thou mayest shame to expresse. But ah Fawnia, love is a Lord, who will commaund by power, and constraine by force. Dorastus, ah Dorastus is the man I love, the woorse is thy hap, and the lesse cause hast thou to hope. Will Eagles catch at flyes, will Cedars stoupe to brambles, or mighty Princes looke at such homely trulles? No, no, thinke this, Dorastus disdaine is greater then thy desire, hee is a Prince respecting his honour, thou a beggars brat forgetting thy calling. Cease then not onely to say, but to thinke to love Dorastus, and dissemble thy love Fawnia, for better it were to dye with griefe, then to live with shame: yet in despight of love I will sigh, to see if I can sigh out love. ⁋ Fawnia somewhat appeasing her griefes with these pithie perswasions, began after her wonted maner to walke about her sheepe, and to keepe them from straying into the corne, suppressing her affection with the due consideration of her base estate, and with the impossibilities of her love, thinking it were frenzy, not fancy, to covet that which the very destinies did deny her to obteine. ⁋ But Dorastus was more impatient in his

33

passions; for love so fiercely assayled him, that neither companie, nor musicke could mittigate his martirdome, but did rather far the more increase his maladie: shame would not let him crave counsaile in this case, nor feare of his Fathers displeasure reveyle it to any secrete friend; but hee was faine to make a Secretarie of himselfe, and to participate his thoughtes with his owne troubled mind. Lingring thus awhile in doubtfull suspence, at last stealing secretely from the court without either men or Page, hee went to see if hee could espie Fawnia walking abroade in the field; but as one having a great deale more skill to retrive the partridge with his spaniels, then to hunt after such a straunge pray, he sought, but was little the better: which crosse lucke drave him into a great choler, that he began to accuse love and fortune. But as he was readie to retire, he sawe Fawnia sitting all alone under the side of a hill, making a garland of such homely flowres as the fields did afoord. This sight so revived his spirites that he drewe nigh, with more judgement to take a view of her singular perfection, which hee found to bee such as in that countrey attyre she stained al the courtlie Dames of Sicilia. While thus he stoode gazing with pearcing lookes on her surpassing beautie, Fawnia cast her eye aside, and spyed Dorastus, with sudden sight made the poore girle to blush, and to die her christal cheeks with a vermilion red; which gave her such a grace, as she seemed farre more beautiful. And with that she rose up, saluting the Prince with such modest curtesies, as he wondred how a country maid could afoord such courtly behaviour. Dorastus, repaying her curtesie with a smiling countenance, began to parlie with her on this manner. ¶ Faire maide (quoth he) either your want is great, or a shepheards life very sweete, that your delight is in such country labors. I can not conceive what pleasure you should take, unless you meane to imitate the nymphes, being yourself so like a Nymph. To put me out of this doubt, shew me what is to be commended in a shepherdes life, and what pleasures you have to countervaile these drudging laboures. ¶ Fawnia with blushing face made him this ready aunswere. Sir, what richer state

34

then content, or what sweeter life then quiet? we shepheards are not borne to honor, nor beholding unto beautie, the less care we have to feare fame or fortune: we count our attire brave inough if warme inough, and our foode dainty, if to suffice nature: our greatest enemie is the wolfe; our onely care in safe keeping our flock: in stead of courtlie ditties we spend the daies with cuntry songs: our amorous conceites are homely thoughtes; delighting as much to talke of Pan and his cuntrey prankes, as Ladies to tell of Venus and her wanton toyes. Our toyle is in shifting the fouldes, and looking to the Lambes, easie labours: oft singing and telling tales, homely pleasures; our greatest welth not to covet, our honor not to climbe, our quiet not to care. Envie looketh not so lowe as shepheards: Shepheards gaze not so high as ambition: we are rich in that we are poore with content, and proud onely in this, that we have no cause to be proud. ⸿ This wittie aunswer of Fawnia so inflamed Dorastus fancy, as he commended him selfe for making so good a choyce, thinking, if her birth were aunswerable to her wit and beauty, that she were a fitte mate for the most famous Prince in the worlde. He therefore beganne to sifte her more narrowely on this manner. ⸿ Fawnia, I see thou art content with Country labours, because thou knowest not Courtly pleasures: I commend thy wit, and pitty thy want: but wilt thou leave thy Fathers Cottage and serve a Courtlie Mistresse? ⸿ Sir (quoth she) beggers ought not to strive against fortune, nor to gaze after honour, least either their fall be greater, or they become blinde. I am borne to toile for the Court, not in the Court, my nature unfit for their nurture: better live then in meane degree, than in high disdaine. ⸿ Well saide, Fawnia (quoth Dorastus) I guesse at thy thoughtes; thou art in love with some Countrey Shephearde. ⸿ No sir (quoth she) shepheards cannot love, that are so simple, and maides may not love that are so young. ⸿ Nay therefore (quoth Dorastus) maides must love, because they are young, for Cupid is a child, and Venus, though olde, is painted with fresh coloures. ⸿ I graunt (quoth she) age may be painted with new shadowes, and youth may have imperfect affections;

35

but what arte concealeth in one, ignorance revealeth in the other. Dorastus seeing Fawnia held him so harde, thought it was vaine so long to beate about the bush: therefore he thought to have given her a fresh charge; but he was prevented by certaine of his men, who missing their maister, came posting to seeke him; seeing that he was gone foorth all alone, yet before they drewe so nie that they might heare their talke, he used these speeches. ❡ Why Fawnia, perhappes I love thee, and then thou must needes yeelde, for thou knowest I can commaund and constraine. Trueth sir (quoth she) but not to love; for constrained love is force, not love: and know this sir, mine honesty is such, as I hadde rather dye then be a concubine even to a King, and my birth is so base as I am unfitte to bee a wife to a poore farmer. Why then (quoth he) thou canst not love Dorastus. Yes saide Fawnia, when Dorastus becomes a shepheard, and with that the presence of his men broke off their parle, so that he went with them to the palace and left Fawnia sitting still on the hill side, who seeing that the night drewe on, shifted her fouldes, and busied her selfe about other worke to drive away such fond fancies as began to trouble her braine. But all this could not prevaile, for the beautie of Dorastus had made such a deepe impression in her heart, as it could not be worne out without cracking, so that she was forced to blame her owne folly in this wise. ❡ Ah Fawnia, why doest thou gaze against the Sunne, or catch at the Winde? starres are to be looked at with the eye, not reacht at with the hande: thoughts are to be measured by Fortunes, not by desires: falles come not by sitting low, but by climing too hie: what then shal al feare to fal, because some happe to fall? No luck commeth by lot, and fortune windeth those threedes which the destinies spin. Thou art favored Fawnia of a prince, and yet thou art so fond to reject desired favours: thou hast deniall at thy tonges end, and desire at thy hearts bottome; a womans fault, to spurne at that with her foote, which she greedily catcheth at with her hand. Thou lovest Dorastus, Fawnia, and yet seemest to lower. Take heede, if hee retire thou wilt repent; for unles

36

hee love, thou canst but dye. Dye then Fawnia; for Dorastus doth but jest: the Lyon never prayeth on the mouse, nor Faulcons stoupe not to dead stales. Sit downe then in sorrow, ceasse to love, and content thy selfe, that Dorastus will vouchsafe to flatter Fawnia, though not to fancy Fawnia. Heigh ho! Ah foole, it were seemelier for thee to whistle as a Shepheard, then to sigh as a lover. And with that she ceassed from these perplexed passions, folding her sheepe, and hying home to her poore Cottage. ❡ But such was the incessant sorrow of Dorastus to thinke on the witte and beautie of Fawnia, and to see how fond hee was being a Prince; and how froward she was being a beggar, then he began to loose his wonted appetite, to looke pale and wan; instead of mirth, to feede on melancholy; for courtly daunces to use cold dumpes; in so much that not onely his owne men, but his father and all the court began to marvaile at his sudden change, thinking that some lingring sickenes had brought him into this state: wherefore he caused Phisitions to come, but Dorastus neither would let them minister, nor so much as suffer them to see his urine; but remained stil so oppressed with these passions, as he feared in him selfe a farther inconvenience. His honor wished him to ceasse from such folly, but Love forced him to follow fancy: yea and in despight of honour, love wonne the conquest, so that his hot desires caused him to find new devises, for hee presently made himselfe a shepheards coate, that he might goe unknowne, and with the lesse suspition to prattle with Fawnia, and conveied it secretly into a thick grove hard joyning to the Pallace, whether finding fit time, and opportunity, he went all alone, and putting off his princely apparel got on those shepheards roabes, and taking a great hooke in his hand (which he had also gotten) he went very anciently [sic] to find out the mistres of his affection: but as he went by the way, seeing himselfe clad in such unseemely ragges, he began to smile at his owne folly, and to reprove his fondnesse, in these tearmes. ❡ Well said Dorastus, thou keepest a right decorum, base desires and homely attires: thy thoughtes are fit for none but a shepheard, and

37

thy apparell such as only become a shepheard. A strange change from a Prince to a pesant! What is it? thy wretched fortune or thy wilful folly? Is it thy cursed destinies? Or thy crooked desires, that appointeth thee this penance? Ah Dorastus thou canst but love, and unlesse thou love, thou art like to perish for love. Yet fond foole, choose flowers, not weedes; Diamondes, not peables; Ladies which may honour thee, not shepheards which may disgrace thee. Venus is painted in silkes, not in ragges; and Cupid treadeth on disdaine, when he reacheth at dignitie. And yet Dorastus shame not at thy shepheards weede: the heavenly Godes have sometime earthly thoughtes: Neptune became a ram, Jupiter a Bul, Apollo a shepheard: they Gods, and yet in love; and thou a man appointed to love. ℂ Devising thus with himselfe, hee drew nigh to the place where Fawnia was keeping her shepe, who casting her eye aside, and seeing such a manerly shepheard, perfectly limmed, and comming with so good a pace, she began halfe to forget Dorastus, and to favor this pretty shepheard, whom she thought shee might both love and obtaine: but as shee was in these thoughts, she perceived then, that it was the yong prince Dorastus, wherfore she rose up and reverently saluted him. Dorastus taking her by the hand, repaied her curtesie with a sweet kisse, and praying her to sit downe by him, he began thus to lay the batterie. ℂ If thou marvell Fawnia at my strange attyre, thou wouldest more muse at my unaccustomed thoughtes: the one disgraceth but my outward shape, the other disturbeth my inward sences. I love Fawnia, and therefore what love liketh I cannot mislike. Fawnia thou hast promised to love, and I hope thou wilt performe no lesse: I have fulfilled thy request, and now thou canst but graunt my desire. Thou wert content to love Dorastus when he ceast to be a Prince and to become a shepheard, and see I have made the change, and therefore not to misse of my choice. ℂ Trueth, quoth Fawnia, but all that weare Cooles are not Monkes: painted Eagles are pictures, not Eagles. Zeusis Grapes were like Grapes, yet shadowes: rich clothing make not princes: nor

38

homely attyre beggers: shepheards are not called shepheardes, because they were hookes and bagges, but that they are borne poore, and live to keepe sheepe; so this attire hath not made Dorastus a shepherd, but to seeme like a shepherd. ❡ Well Fawnia, answered Dorastus, were I a shepherd, I could not but like thee, and being a prince I am forst to love thee. Take heed Fawnia be not proud of beauties painting, for it is a flower that fadeth in the blossome. Those which disdayne in youth are despised in age: Beauties shadowes are trickt up with times colours, which being set to drie in the sunne are stained with the sunne, scarce pleasing the sight ere they beginne not to be worth the sight, not much unlike the herbe Ephemeron, which flourisheth in the morning and is withered before the sunne setting: if my desire were against lawe, thou mightest justly deny me by reason; but I love thee Fawnia, not to misuse thee as a Concubine, but to use thee as my wife: I can promise no more, and meane to performe no lesse. ❡ Fawnia hearing this solemne protestation of Dorastus, could no longer withstand the assault, but yeelded up the forte in these friendly tearmes. ❡ Ah Dorastus, I shame to expresse that thou forcest me with thy sugred speeche to confesse: my base birth causeth the one, and thy high dignities the other. Beggars thoughts ought not to reach so far as Kings, and yet my desires reach as high as Princes. I dare not say, Dorastus, I love thee, because I am a shepherd; but the Gods know I have honored Dorastus (pardon if I say amisse) yea and loved Dorastus with such dutiful affection as Fawnia can performe, or Dorastus desire: I yeeld, not overcome with prayers, but with love, resting Dorastus handmaid ready to obey his wil, if no prejudice at all to his honour, nor to my credit. ❡ Dorastus hearing this freendly conclusion of Fawnia embraced her in his armes, swearing that neither distance, time, nor adverse fortune should diminish his affection: but that in despight of the destinies he would remaine loyall unto death. Having thus plight their troath each to other, seeing they could not have the full fruition of their love in Sycilia, for that Egistus consent

39

woulde never bee graunted to so meane a match, Dorastus determined, assone as time and oportunitie would give them leave, to provide a great masse of money, and many rich and costly jewels, for the easier cariage, and then to transporte themselves and their treasure into Italy, where they should leade a contented life, until such time as either he could be reconciled to his Father, or els by sucession come to the Kingdome. This devise was greatly praysed of Fawnia, for she feared if the King his father should but heare of the contract, that his furie would be such as no lesse than death would stand for payment: she therefore tould him, that delay bred daunger: that many mishaps did fall out betweene the cup and the lip, and that to avoid danger, it were best with as much speed as might be to pass out of Sycilia, least fortune might prevent their pretence with some newe despight: Dorastus, whom love pricked forward with desire, promised to dispatch his affaires with as great hast, as either time or oportunitie would geve him leave: and so resting upon this point, after many imbracings and sweete kisses they departed, ⟨ Dorastus having taken his leave of his best beloved Fawnia, went to the Grove where hee had his rich apparel, and there uncasing himself as secretly as might be, hiding up his shepheards attire, till occasion should serve againe to use it: he went to the pallace, shewing by his merrie countenaunce, that either the state of his body was amended, or the case of his minde greatly redressed: Fawnia poore soule was no less joyful, that being a shepheard, fortune had favoured her so, as to reward her with the love of a Prince, hoping in time to be advaunced from the daughter of a poore farmer to be the wife of a riche King: so that she thought every houre a yeere, till by their departure they might prevent danger, not ceasing still to goe every daye to her sheepe, not so much for the care of her flock, as for the desire she had to see her love and Lord Dorastus: who oftentimes, when oportunitie would serve, repaired thither to feede his fancy with the sweet content of Fawnias presence: and although he never went to visit her, but in his

40

shepheards ragges, yet his ofte repaire made him not onely suspected, but knowne to divers of their neighbours: who for the good will they bare to old Porrus, tould him secretly of the matter, wishing him to keepe his daughter at home, least she went so ofte to the field that she brought him home a yong sonne: for they feared that Fawnia being so beautifull, the yong prince would allure her to folly. Porrus was stricken into a dump at these newes, so that thanking his neighboures for their good will: he hyed him home to his wife, and calling her aside, wringing his handes and shedding foorth teares, he brake the matter to her in these tearmes. ℭ I am afraid wife, that my daughter Fawnia hath made her selfe so fine, that she will buy repentance too deare. I heare newes, which if they be true, some will wish they had not proved true. It is tould me by my neighbours, that Dorastus the Kinges sonne begins to looke at our daughter Fawnia; which if it be so, I will not geve her a halfepeny for her honestie at the yeeres end. I tell thee wife, nowadaies beautie is a great stale to trap yong men, and faire wordes and sweete promises are two great enemies to a maydens honestie: and thou knowest where poore men intreate, and cannot obtaine, there Princes may commaund, and wil obtaine. Though Kings sonnes daunce in nettes, they may not be seene: but poore mens faultes are spied at a little hole: Well, it is a hard case where Kinges lustes are lawes, and that they should binde poore men to that, which they themselves wilfully breake. ℭ Peace husband (quoth his wife) take heede what you say: speake no more than you should, least you heare what you would not: great streames are to be stopped by sleight, not by force: and princes to be perswaded by submission, not by rigor: doe what you can, but no more than you may, least in saving Fawnias mayden-head, you loose your owne head. Take heede I say, it is ill jesting with edged tooles, and bad sporting with Kinges. The Wolfe had his skinne puld over his eares for but looking into the Lions den. Tush wife (quoth he) thou speakest like a foole, if the King should knowe that Dorastus had begotten our daughter with

41

childe (as I feare it will fall out little better) the Kings
furie would be such as no doubt we should both loose our
goodes and lives: necessitie therefore hath no lawe, and I
will prevent this mischiefe with a newe devise that is come
into my head, which shall neither offend the King, nor displease Dorastus. I meane to take the chaine and the jewels
that I found with Fawnia, and carrie them to the King, let-
ting him then to understand how she is none of my daughter, but that I found her beaten up with the water alone in
a little boate wrapped in a riche Mantle, wherein was in-
closed this treasure. By this meanes I hope the King will
take Fawnia into his service, and we whatsoever chaunceth
shal be blamelesse. This device pleased the good wife very
well, so that they determined, assoone as they might know
the King at leisure, to make him privie to this case. ℂ In
the meane time Dorastus was not slacke in his affaires, but
applyed his matters with such diligence, that he provided
all thinges fitte for their journey. Treasure and Jewels he
had gotten great store, thincking there was no better friend
then money in a strange countrey: rich attire he had provided for Fawnia, and, because he could not bring the matter to passe without the helpe and advice of some one, he
made an old servant of his called Capnio, who had served
him from his childhood, privie to his affaires: who seeing
no perswasions could prevaile to divert him from his setled
determination, gave his consent and dealt so secretly in the
cause, that within short space hee had gotten a ship ready
for their passage: the Mariners seeing a fit gale of winde for
their purpose, wished Capnio to make no delayes, least if
they pretermitted this good weather, they might stay long
ere they had such a fayre winde. Capnio fearing that his
negligence should hinder the journey, in the night time con-
veyed the trunckes full of treasure into the shippe, and by
secrette meanes let Fawnia understand, that the next morning they meant to depart: she upon this newes slept verie
little that night, but gotte up very early, and wente to her
sheepe, looking every minute when she should see Dorastus,
who taried not long, for feare delay might breede daunger,

42

but came as fast as he could gallop, and without any great circumstance took Fawnia up behinde him and rode to the haven, where the shippe lay, which was not three quarters of a mile distant from that place. He no sooner came there, but the Marriners were readie with their Cockboate to set them aboard, where being coucht together in a Cabben they past away the time in recounting their old loves, til their man Capnio should come. Porrus who had heard that this morning the King would go abroad to take the ayre, called in haste to his wife to bring him his holyday hose and his best Iacket, that he might goe like an honest substantiall man to tell his tale. His wife a good cleanly wenche, brought him all things fitte, and spungd him up very handsomlie, giving him the chaines and Iewels in a little boxe, which Porrus for the more safety put in his bosom. Having thus all his trinkets in readines, taking his staffe in his hand he bad his wife kisse him for good lucke, and so hee went towards the Pallace. But as he was going, fortune (who meant to showe him a little false play) prevented his purpose in this wise. ⁋ He met by chaunce in his way Capnio, who trudging as fast as he could with a little coffer under his arme to the ship, and spying Porrus whome he knewe to be Fawnias Father, going towardes the Pallace, being a wylie fellow, began to doubt the worst, and therefore crost him the way, and askt him whither he was going so earely this morning. Porrus (who knew by his face that he was one of the Court) meaning simply, told him that the Kings son Dorastus dealt hardly with him; for he had but one daughter who was a little Beautifull, and that his neigh-boures told him the young Prince had allured her to folly, he went therefore now to complaine to the King how greatly he was abused. ⁋ Capnio (who straight way smelt the whole matter) began to soth him in his talke, and said that Doras-tus dealt not like a Prince to spoyle any poore manes daugh-ter in that sort: he therefore would doe the best for him he could, because he knew he was an honest man. But (quoth Capnio) you lose your labour in going to the Pallace, for the King meanes this day to take the aire of the Sea, and to goe

43

aboord of a shippe that lies in the haven. I am going before, you see, to provide all things in redinesse, and if you
will follow my counsaile, turne back with me to the haven,
where I will set you in such a fitte place as you may speake
to the King at your pleasure. Porrus giving credit to Cap-
nios smooth tale, gave him a thousand thanks for his frendly
advise, and went with him to the haven, making all the way
his complaintes of Dorastus, yet concealing secretlie the
chaine and the Jewels. Assone as they were come to the
Sea side, the marriners seeing Capnio, came a land with
their cock-boate, who still dissembling the matter, demaunded of Porrus if he would go see the ship? who unwilling and fearing the worst, because he was not well acquainted with Capnio, made his excuse that he could not
brooke the Sea, therefore would not trouble him. ⁋ Capnio
seeing that by faire meanes hee could not get him aboord,
commaunded the mariners that by violence they should
carrie him into the shippe, who like sturdy knaves hoisted
the poore shepheard on their backes, and bearing him to
the boate, lanched from the land. ⁋ Porrus seeing himselfe so cunningly betraied durst not crie out, for hee sawe
it would not prevaile, but began to intreate Capnio and the
mariners to be good to him, and to pittie his estate, hee was
but a poore man that lived by his labour: they laughing to
see the shepheard so afraide, made as much haste as they
could, and set him aboorde. Porrus was no sooner in the
shippe, but he saw Dorastus walking with Fawnia, yet he
scarse knew her: for she had attired her selfe in riche apparell, which so increased her beauty, that shee resembled
rather an Angell then a mortall creature. ⁋ Dorastus and
Fawnia, were halfe astonished to see the olde shepherd,
marvailing greatly what wind had brought him thither, til
Capnio told them al the whole discourse; how Porrus was
going to make his complaint to the King, if by pollicie he
had not prevented him, and therefore now sith he was
aboord, for the avoiding of further danger, it were best to
carrie him into Italy. ⁋ Dorastus praised greatly his mans
devise, and allowed of his counsaile; but Fawnia (who stil

44

feared Porrus, as her father) began to blush for shame, that by her meanes he should either incure daunger or displeasure. ⁋ The old shephard hearing this hard sentence, that he should on such a sodaine be caried from his Wife, his country, and kinsfolke, into a forraine Lande amongst straungers, began with bitter teares to make his complaint, and on his knees to intreate Dorastus, that pardoning his unadvised folly he would give him leave to goe home; swearing that hee would keepe all thinges as secret as they could wish. But these protestations could not prevaile, although Fawnia intreated Dorastus very earnestly, but the mariners hoisting their maine sailes waied ankers, and hailed into the deepe, where we leave them to the favour of the wind and seas, and returne to Egistus. ⁋ Who having appointed this day to hunt in one of his Forrests, called for his sonne Dorastus to go sport himselfe, because hee saw that of late hee began to loure; but his men made answer that hee was gone abroade none knew whither, except he were gone to the grove to walke all alone, as his custome was to doe every day. ⁋ The King willing to waken him out of his dumpes sent one of his men to goe seeke him, but in vaine, for at last he returned, but finde him he could not, so that the King went himselfe to goe see the sport; where passing away the day, returning at night from hunting, hee asked for his sonne, but he could not be heard of, which drave the King into a great choler: where upon most of his Noblemen and other Courtiers, poasted abroad to seek him, but they could not heare of him through all Sicilia, onely they missed Capnio his man, which againe made the King suspect that hee was not gone farre. ⁋ Two or three daies being passed, and no newes heard of Dorastus, Egistus began to feare that he was devoured with some wilde beastes, and upon that made out a great troupe of men to go seeke him; who coasted through all the Country, and searched in everie daungerous and secrete place, untill at last they mette with a Fisherman that was sitting in a little covert hard by the sea side mending his nettes, when Dorastus and Fawnia tooke shipping;

45

who being examined if he either knewe or heard where the Kings Sonne was, without any secrecie at all revealed the whole matter, how he was sayled two dayes past, and had in his company his man Capnio, Porrus and his faire Daughter Fawnia. This heavie newes was presently caryed to the King, who halfe dead for sorrow commaunded Porrus wife to bee sent for: she being come to the Pallace, after due examination, confessed that her neighbours had oft told her that the Kings Sonne was too familier with Fawnia, her Daughter: whereuppon, her husband fearing the worst, about two dayes past (hearing the King should goe an hunting) rose earely in the morning and went to make his complaint, but since she neither hearde of him, nor saw him. Egistus perceiving the womans unfeyned simplicity, let her depart without incurring further displeasure, conceiving such secret greefe for his Sonnes recklesse follie, that he had so forgotten his honour and parentage, by so base a choise to dishonor his Father, and discredit himselfe, that with very care and thought be fel into a quartan fever, which was so unfit for his aged yeeres and complexion, that he became so weake, as the Phisitions would graunt him no life. ❡ But his sonne Dorastus little regarded either father, countrie, or Kingdome in respect of his Lady Fawnia, for fortune smyling on this young novice, lent him so lucky a gale of winde, for the space of a day and a night, that the maryners lay and slept upon the hatches; but on the next morning about the breake of the day, the aire began to be overcast, the winds to rise, the seas to swel, yea presently there arose such a fearfull tempest, as the ship was in danger to be swallowed up with every sea, the maine mast with the violence of the wind was thrown over boord, the sayles were torne, the tacklings went in sunder, the storme raging still so furiously that poore Fawnia was almost dead for feare, but that she was greatly comforted with the presence of Dorastus. The tempest continued three dayes, at which time the Mariners everie minute looked for death, and the aire was so darkned with cloudes that the Maister could not tell by his compasse in what Coast

46

they were. But upon the fourth day about ten of the clocke, the wind began to cease, the sea to wax calme, and the sky to be cleare, and the Mariners descryed the coast of Bohemia, shooting of their ordnance for joy that they had escaped such a fearefull tempest. ⁊ Dorastus hearing that they were arrived at some harbour, sweetly kissed Fawnia, and bad her be of good cheare: when they tolde him that the port belonged unto the cheife Cittie of Bohemia where Pandosto kept his Court, Dorastus began to be sad, knowing that his Father hated no man so much as Pandosto, and that the King himself had sought secretly to betray Egistus: this considered, he was halfe afraide to goe on land, but that Capnio counselled him to chaunge his name and his countrey, until such time as they could get some other barke to transport them into Italy. Dorastus liking this devise made his case privy to the Marriners, rewarding them bountifully for their paines, and charging them to saye that he was a Gentleman of Trapalonia called Meleagrus. The shipmen willing to shew what friendship they could to Dorastus, promised to be as secret as they could, or hee might wish, and uppon this they landed in a little village a mile distant from the Citie, where after they had rested a day, thinking to make provision for their mariage; the fame of Fawnias beauty was spread throughout all the Citie, so that it came to the eares of Pandosto; who then being about the age of fifty, had notwithstanding yong and freshe affections: so that he desired greatly to see Fawnia, and to bring this matter the better to passe, hearing they had but one man, and how they rested at a very homely house; he caused them to be apprehended as spies, and sent a dozen of his garde to take them: who being come to their lodging, tolde them the Kings message. Dorastus no whit dismayed, accompanied with Fawnia and Capnio, went to the court (for they left Porrus to keepe the stuffe) who being admitted to the Kings presence, Dorastus and Fawnia with humble obedience saluted his majestie. ⁊ Pandosto amased at the singular perfection of Fawnia, stood halfe astonished, viewing her beauty, so that he had almost forgot

47

himselfe what hee had to doe: at last with stearne countenance he demaunded their names, and of what countrey they were, and what caused them to land in Bohemia, Sir (quoth Dorastus) know that my name Meleagrus is a Knight borne and brought up in Trapalonia, and this gentlewoman, whom I meane to take to my wife is an Italian borne in Padua, from whence I have now brought her. The Cause I have so small a trayne with me is for that her friends unwilling to consent, I intended secretly to convey her into Trapalonia; whither as I was sailing, by distresse of weather I was driven into these coasts: thus have you heard my name, my country, and the cause of my voiage. Pandosto starting from his seat as one in choller, made this rough reply. ⁋ Meleagrus, I feare this smooth tale hath but small trueth, and that thou coverest a foule skin with faire paintings. No doubt this Ladie by her grace and beauty is of her degree more meete for a mighty Prince, then for a simple knight, and thou like a perjured traitour hath bereft her of her parents, to their present griefe, and her insuing sorrow. Till therefore I heare more of her parentage and of thy calling, I wil stay you both here in Bohemia. ⁋ Dorastus, in whome rested nothing but Kingly valor, was not able to suffer the reproches of Pandosto, but that he made him this answer. ⁋ It is not meete for a King, without due proofe to appeach any man of ill behaviour, nor upon suspition to inferre beleefe: straungers ought to bee entertained with courtesie, not to bee intreated with crueltie, least being forced by want to put up injuries: the Gods revenge their cause with rigor. ⁋ Pandosto hearing Dorastus utter these wordes, commaunded that he should straight be committed to prison, untill such time as they heard further of his pleasure, but as for Fawnia, he charged that she should be entertained in the Court, with such curtesie as belonged to a straunger and her calling. The rest of the shipmen he put into the dungeon. ⁋ Having thus hardly handled the supposed Trapalonians Pandosto contrarie to his aged yeares began to be somewhat tickled with the beauty of Fawnia, in so much that hee could take no rest, but cast

48

in his old head a thousand new devises: at last he fell into these thoughtes. ⟨How art thou pestred Pandosto with fresh affections, and unfitte fancies, wishing to possesse with an unwilling mynd, and a hot desire troubled with a could disdaine? Shall thy mynde yeeld in age to that thou hast resisted in youth? Peace Pandosto, blabbe not out that which thou maiest be ashamed to reveale to thy self. Ah Fawnia is beautifull, and it is not for thine honour (fond foole) to name her that is thy Captive, and another mans Concubine. Alas, I reach at that with my hand which my hart would fain refuse; playing like the bird Ibys in Egipt, which hateth Serpents, yet feedeth on their egges. Tush, hot desires turne oftentimes to colde disdaine: Love is brittle, where appetite, not reason, beares the sway: Kinges thoughtes ought not to climbe so high as the heavens, but to looke no lower then honour: better it is to pecke at the starres with the young Eagles, then to pray on dead carkasses with the Vulture: tis more honourable for Pandosto to dye by concealing Love, than to enjoy such unfitte Love. Dooth Pandosto then love? Yea: whome? A maide unknowne, yea, and perhapps immodest, stragled out of her owne countrie; beautifull, but not therefore chast; comely in bodie, but perhappes crooked in minde. Cease then Pandosto to looke at Fawnia, much lesse to love her: be not overtaken with a womans beauty, whose eyes are framed by arte to inamour, whose hearte is framed by nature to inchaunt, whose false teares knowe their true times, and whose sweete wordes pearce deeper then sharpe swordes. ⟨Here Pandosto ceased from his talke, but not from his love: although he sought by reason and wisedome to suppresse this franticke affection: yet he could take no rest, the beautie of Fawnia had made such a deepe impression in his heart. But on a day walking abroad into a Parke which was hard adjoyning to his house, he sent by one of his servants for Fawnia, unto whome he uttered these wordes. ⟨Fawnia, I commend thy beauty and wit, and now pittie thy distresse and want; but if thou wilt forsake Sir Meleagrus, whose poverty, though a Knight, is not able to

49

maintaine an estate aunswerable to thy beauty, and yeld thy consent to Pandosto, I will both increase thee with dignities and riches. No sir, answered Fawnia; Meleagrus is a knight that hath wonne me by love, and none but he shal weare me: his sinister mischance shall not diminishe my affection, but rather increase my good will: thinke not though your Grace had imprisoned him without cause, that feare shall make mee yeeld my consent: I had rather be Meleagrus wife, and a begger, then live in plenty, and be Pandostos Concubine. Pandosto hearing the assured aunswere of Fawnia, would, notwithstanding, prosecute his suite to the uttermost; seeking with faire wordes and great promises to scale the fort of her chastitie, swearing that if she would graunt to his desire Meleagrus should not only be set at libertie, but honored in his courte amongst his Nobles: but these alluring baytes could not entise her minde from the love of her newe betrothed mate Meleagrus; which Pandosto seeing, he left her alone for that time to consider more of the demaund. Fawnia being alone by her selfe, began to enter into these solitarie meditations ❡ Ah infortunate Fawnia thou seest to desire above fortune, is to strive against the Gods, and Fortune. Who gazeth at the sunne weakeneth his sight: they which stare at the skie, fall ofte into deepe pits: haddest thou rested content to have bene a shepheard, thou needest not to have feared mischaunce: better had it bene for thee, by sitting lowe, to have had quiet, then by climing high to have fallen into miserie. But alas I feare not mine owne daunger, but Dorastus displeasure. Ah sweete Dorastus, thou art a Prince, but now a prisoner, by too much love procuring thine owne losse: haddest thou not loved Fawnia thou haddest bene fortunate: shall I then bee false to him that hath forsaken Kingdomes for my cause? no, would my death might deliver him, so mine honor might be preserved. With that fetching a deepe sigh, she ceased from her complaints, and went againe to the Pallace, injoying a libertie without content, and profered pleasure with smal joy. But poore Dorastus lay all this while in close prison, being

50

pinched with a hard restraint, and pained with the burden of colde, and heavie Irons, sorrowing sometimes that his fond affection had procured him this mishappe, that by the disobedience of his parentes, he had wrought his owne despright: an other while cursing the Gods and fortune, that they should crosse him with such sinister chaunce: uttering at last his passions in these words. ❡ Ah unfortunate wretch borne to mishappe, now thy folly hath his desert: art thou not worthie for thy base minde to have bad fortune? could the destinies favour thee, which hast forgot thine honor and dignities? wil not the Gods plague him with despight that payneth his father with disobedience? Oh Gods, if any favour or justice be left, plague me, but favour poore Fawnia, and shrowd her from the tirannies of wretched Pandosto, but let my death free her from mishap, and then welcome death. Dorastus payned with these heavie passions, sorrowed and sighed, but in vaine, for which he used the more patience. But againe to Pandosto, who broyling at the heat of unlawfull lust, coulde take no rest but still felt his minde disquieted with his new love, so that his nobles and subjectes marveyled greatly at this sudaine alteration, not being able to conjecture the cause of this his continued care. Pandosto thinking every hower a yeare til he had talked once againe with Fawnia, sent for her secretly into his chamber, whither though Fawnia unwillingly comming, Pandosto entertained her very courteously using these familiar speaches, which Fawnia answered as shortly in this wise.

PANDOSTO.

❡ Fawnia are you become lesse wilfull and more wise, to preferre the love of a King before the liking of a poore Knight? I thinke ere this you thinke it is better to be favoured of a King then of a subject.

FAWNIA.

❡ Pandosto, the body is subject to victories, but the minde not to be subdued by conquest, honesty is to be preferred

51

before honour, and a dramme of faith weigheth downe a tunne of gold. I have promised Meleagrus to love, and will performe no lesse.

PANDOSTO.

❡ Fawnia, I know thou art not so unwise in thy choice, as to refuse the offer of a King, nor so ingrateful as to dispise a good turne: thou art now in that place where I may commaunde, and yet thou seest I intreate: my power is such as I may compell by force, and yet I sue by prayers: Yeelde Fawnia thy love to him which burneth in thy love: Meleagrus shall be set free, thy countrymen discharged, and thou both loved and honoured.

FAWNIA.

❡ I see Pandosto, where lust ruleth it is a miserable thing to be a virgin, but know this, that I will alwaies preferre fame before life, and rather choose death then dishonour.

❡ Pandosto seeing that there was in Fawnia a determinate courage to love Meleagrus, and a resolution without feare to hate him, flong away from her in a rage: swearing if in shorte time she would not be wonne with reason; he would forget all courtesie, and compel her to graunt by rigour: but these threatning wordes no whit dismayed Fawnia; but that she still both dispited and dispised Pandosto. While thus these two lovers strove, the one to winne love the other to live in hate: Egistus heard certaine newes by the Merchauntes of Bohemia, that his sonne Dorastus was imprisoned by Pandosto, which made him feare greatly that his sonne should be but hardly entreated: yet considering that Bellaria and hee was cleared by the Oracle of Apóllo from that crime wherewith Pandosto had unjustly charged him, hee thought best to send with all speed to Pandosto, that he should set free his sonne Dorastus, and put to death Fawnia and her father Porrus: finding this by the advise of Counsaile the speediest remedy to release his sonne, he caused presently too of his shippes to be rigged, and thoroughly

52

furnished with provision of men and victuals, and sent divers of his men and nobles Embassadoures into Bohemia; who willing to obey their King, and relieve their yong Prince: made no delayes, for feare of danger, but with as much speed as might be, sailed towards Bohemia: the winde and seas favored them greatly, which made them hope of some good happe, for within three daies they were landed: which Pandosto no soner heard of their arrivall, but hee in person went to meete them, intreating them with such sumptuous and familiar courtesie, that they might well perceive how sory he was for the former injuries hee had offered to their King, and how willing (if it might be) to make amendes. ❡ As Pandosto made report to them, how one Maleagrus, a Knight of Trapolonia, was lately arived with a Lady called Fawnia in his land, comming very suspitiously, accompanied onely with one servant, and an olde shepheard. The Embassadours perceived by the halfe, what the whole tale ment, and began to conjecture, that it was Dorastus, who for feare to bee knowne, had chaunged his name: but dissembling the matter, they shortly arived at the Court, where after they had bin verie solemnly and sumptuously feasted, the noble men of Sicilia being gathered togither, they made reporte of their Embassage: where they certified Pandosto that Meleagrus was sonne and heire to the King Egistus, and that his name was Dorastus: how contrarie to the Kings minde he had privily convaied away that Fawnia, intending to marrie her, being but daughter to that poore shepheard Porrus: whereupon the Kings request was that Capnio, Fawnia, and Porrus, might bee murthered and put to death, and that his sonne Dorastus might be sent home in safetie. Pandosto having attentively and with great mervaile heard their Embassage, willing to reconcile himselfe to Egistus, and to shew him how greatly he esteemed his favour: although love and fancy forbad him to hurt Fawnia, yet in despight of love hee determined to execute Egistus will without mercy; and therefore he presently sent for Dorastus out of prison, who mervailing at this unlooked for curtesie, found at his

53

comming to the Kings presence, that which he least doubted of, his fathers Embassadours: who no sooner sawe him, but with great reverence they honored him: and Pandosto embracing Dorastus, set him by him very lovingly in a chaire of estate. Dorastus ashamed that his follie was bewraied, sate a long time as one in a muse, til Pandosto told him the summe of his Fathers embassage: which he had no sooner heard, but he was toucht at the quicke, for the cruell sentence that was pronounced against Fawnia: but neither could his sorrow nor perswasions prevaile, for Pandosto commaunded that Fawnia, Porrus, and Capnio, should bee brought to his presence; who were no sooner come, but Pandosto having his former love turned to a disdainfull hate, began to rage against Fawnia in these tearmes. ❡ Thou disdainfull vassal, thou currish kite, assigned by the destinies to base fortune, and yet with an aspiring minde gazing after honour: how durst thou presume, being a beggar, to match with a Prince? By thy alluring lookes to inchant the sonne of a King to leave his owne countrie to fulfill thy disordinate lusts? O despightfull minde, a proud heart in a beggar is not unlike to a great fire in a smal cottage, which warmeth not the house, but burneth it: assure thy selfe that thou shalt die, and thou old doating foole, whose follie hath bene such, as to suffer thy daughter to reach above thy fortune; looke for no other meede, but the like punishment. But Capnio, thou which hast betrayed the King, and hast consented to the unlawfull lust of thy Lord and maister, I know not how justly I may plague thee: death is too easie a punishment for thy falsehood, and to live (if not in extreme miserie) were not to shew thee equitie. I therefore award that thou shall have thine eyes put out, and continually while thou diest, grinde in a mil like a brute beast. The feare of death brought a sorrowfull silence upon Fawnia and Capnio, but Porrus seeing no hope of life, burst forth into these speeches. ❡ Pandosto, and ye noble Embassadours of Sicilia, seeing without cause I am condemned to die; I am yet glad I have opportunitie to disburden my conscience before my death: I will tel you as much as I know, and yet no more than is true: whereas I am accused that I have bene a supporter of Fawnias pride, and shee disdained as a vilde begger, so it is that I am neither Father unto her, nor she daughter unto me. For so it happened that I being a poore shepheard in Sicilia, living by keeping others mens flockes; one of my sheepe straying downe to the sea side, as I went to seeke her, I saw a little boat driven upon the shoare, wherein I found a babe of sixe daies olde, wrapped in a mantle of skarlet, having about the necke this chaine: I pittying the child, and desirous of the treasure, carried it home to my wife, who with great-care nursed it up, and set it to keepe sheepe. Here is the chaine and the Jewels, and this Fawnia is the childe whome I found in the boate, what shee is, or of what parentage I knowe not, but this I am assured that shee is none of mine. ❧ Pandosto would scarce suffer him to tell out his tale, but that he en- quired the time of the yeere, the manner of the boate, and other circumstaunces, which when he found agreeing to his count, he sodainelie leapt from his seate, and kissed Fawnia, wetting her tender cheeks with his teares, and crying my daughter Fawnia, ah sweete Fawnia, I am thy Father, Fawnia. This sodaine passion of the King drave them all into a maze, especially Fawnia and Dorastus. But when the King had breathed himselfe a while in this newe joy, he rehearsed before the Embassadours the whole matter, how hee hadde entreated his wife Bellaria for jealousie, and that this was the childe whome hee sent to floate in the seas. ❧ Fawnia was not more joyfull that she had found such a Father, then Dorastus was glad he should get such a wife. The Embassadors rejoyced that their yong prince had made such a choice, that those Kingdomes, which through enmitie had long time bin dissevered, should now through perpetual amitie be united and reconciled. The Citizens and subjects of Bohemia (hearing that the King had found againe his Daughter, which was supposed dead, joyfull that there was an heire apparent to his Kingdome) made Bonfires and showes throughout the Cittie. The Courtiers and Knights appointed Justs and Turneis to signifie their willing mindes in gratifying the Kings hap. ℂ Eighteene daies being past in these princely sports, Pandosto willing to recompence old Porrus, of a shepheard made him a Knight: which done, providing a sufficient Navie to receive him and his retinue, accompanied with Dorastus, Fawnia, and the Sicilian Embassadours, he sailed towards Sycilia, where he was most princelie entertained by Egistus; who hearing this comicall event, rejoyced greatly at his sonnes good happe, and without delay (to the perpetuall joy of the two yong Lovers) celebrated the marriage: which was no sooner ended, but Pandosto (calling to mind how first he betraied his friend Egistus, how his jealousie was the cause of Bellarias death, that contrarie to the law of nature hee had lusted after his owne Daughter) moved with these desperate thoughts, he fell into a melancholie fit, and to close up the Comedie with a Tragicall stratageme, he slewe himselfe, whose death being many daies bewailed of Fawnia, Dorastus, and his deere friend Egistus, Dorastus taking his leave of his father, went with his wife and the dead corps into Bohemia, where after they were sumptuouslie intoombed, Dorastus ended his daies in contented quiet.

FINIS.

HERE ENDS PANDOSTO, OR THE HISTORIE OF
DORASTUS AND FAWNIA, BY ROBERT GREENE.

ONE HUNDRED AND SIXTY COPIES HAVE BEEN
PRINTED FROM THE EDITION OF 1588. PRINTED
AND SOLD BY CLARKE CONWELL AT THE ELSTON
PRESS, NEW ROCHELLE, NEW YORK. FINISHED
THIS SIXTEENTH DAY OF OCTOBER, IN THE YEAR

MDCCCCII

Lightning Source UK Ltd.
Milton Keynes UK
UKOW021843250912

199607UK00005B/13/P